Tiffany Rolls On

WHO chains YOU .com PUBLISHING

Stephanie Itle-Clark

Illustrated by Rhonda Van

Published by Who Chains You Books
P.O. Box 581
Amissville, VA 20106
WhoChainsYou.com

Written by Stephanie Itle-Clark
Illustrated by Rhonda Van

ISBN 13: 978-1-946044-44-0

Printed in the United States of America

First Edition

For Chris, the definition
of determination and my
inspiration to always say
YES to the next adventure;
for Tiffany, I will never forget.

I love to go for walks and on new adventures with my family and my best friend Pippen. When I run I feel the wind in my fur and against my ears. Nothing can slow me down.

My family gives me plenty of food and water, plus a lot of love. I have a soft bed that's all mine. They even taught me new things, like how to shake paws. And they take me for bike rides in my special dog basket. This is a great adventure for me because we go really fast—even faster than I can run!

My life was not always so much fun. I used to live in a dark and crowded place. My mother and brother lived with me in a tiny box with a hard metal floor. There were many other dogs in tiny boxes in the gloomy building, too.

It was loud, hot, and it smelled bad in that place. I couldn't run or play. It was so crowded that it was hard to find room to lie down, and sometimes I would be stuck in one corner for hours. It hurt for me to walk on the metal wire floor.

I got my legs stuck in the holes in the floor once and couldn't move. I was tired and scared, and my mother and brother couldn't help me. I was trapped there for a long time.

One day a woman in blue opened the tiny box and picked me up. She got my legs out of the wire floor and said, "Little dog, your life is about to change!" She also took my mother and brother—and all of the other dogs, too—away from that dark and gloomy place. I was very tired, but I liked her and licked her face!

The woman, named Ashley, took me to the animal doctor—she called her a veterinarian. The doctor said I couldn't walk or run because I had weak back legs. My muscles weren't strong, and the wire floor had hurt my back feet. I would never be able to run like the other dogs.

Ashley snuggled me and said, "Even if your muscles are weak, your spirit is strong. The perfect family will adopt you." While we waited for the perfect family to find me, Ashley fostered me at her house and helped me get stronger. We played lots of games—Ashley called this exercise.

Ashley woke me early the first morning at her house. "Get up, pup, it's time to do your exercises," she said. I didn't like the exercises in the beginning because they were hard and I got very tired. Some mornings I would hide under my bed because I didn't want to do them. But soon my front legs grew stronger, and I could use my good legs to move around. I liked being able to explore and go outside in the grass. The grass felt so nice, and I rolled and rolled, enjoying my freedom.

And Ashley was right—the perfect family did find me! A family saw me on an adoption website and wanted to meet me. They said I was just right for them, even if my back legs were not strong. They called me Tiffany and promised to love me forever! Now I get good food and water every single day, lots of toys and belly rubs, and a safe place to live. And they bought me a brand-new collar and ID tag so everyone would know I was part of their family!

My family and my new friend Pippen taught me how to play with toys and how to sun myself in the yard. I kept doing my exercises, but I still couldn't run with my friend because of my weak muscles. Sometimes I got upset that I wasn't the same as the other dogs.

One day my family told me they had a surprise for me. They took me to a special place and got me wheels of my very own! I put my weak back legs in the wheelchair straps, and I used my strong front legs to walk. It took lots of practice, and at first I bumped into things. But I'm a fast learner, and pretty soon I was zooming around. My family clapped and cheered when I flew by, yelling "Great job, Tiffany!" They said they were very proud of me.

Now I always want to go for a walk, and I yip in excitement when my family says, "Let's get your wheels, girl."

In my wheels I can play and run really fast. Sometimes I'm even faster than Pippen!

I may not run just like the other dogs, but in my wheels and with my family, I can do anything.

Resources for Parents and Educators

What is a Puppy Mill?

Puppy mills are high-volume dog breeding facilities where profit outweighs the care of the dogs. Mother and father dogs live in cramped cages with poor sanitation, no exercise or socialization, and little or no veterinary care, causing many of the puppies to suffer from a variety of health issues. The parent dogs are discarded when they can no longer breed. Puppy mills often sell puppies in pet stores, online, or directly to the public. It is estimated by The Humane Society of the United States that as of 2019 there are at least 10,000 puppy mills in the United States.

Educational Resources

There are many resources to expand the conversation about puppy mills with students and to support development of empathy.

The author's organization, the Academy of Prosocial Learning, offers free downloadable curriculums and lesson plans including the *Pawsitive Empathy* curriculums. Activities in *Pawsitive Empathy* engage students in critical thinking and empathy development in the classroom.

Learn more at
www.prosocialacademy.org/resources

About the Author

Stephanie Itle-Clark is a former public-school developmental reading teacher, and the founder and president of the Academy of Prosocial Learning, where she supports prosocial and empathy education and provides resources and professional development for educators. She lives in Pennsylvania with her husband and their pack of tiny rescue dogs.

About the Illustrator

Rhonda Van is an artist, wildlife rehabber, and lifelong animal lover. She particularly adores jackrabbits, squirrels, her animal companions, Shark Week, vegan dinners in Santa Cruz, and her husband Tony. Rhonda has been drawing forever, but only got deeper into illustration after she started drawing the wildlife friends she cares for. Rhonda is the illustrator of *Spittin' Kitten's Speed-Away*, and *Tiffany Rolls On.*

Love this book? Please consider giving *Tiffany Rolls On* a review on Amazon and other venues. Your reviews mean the world to our authors. Thank you!

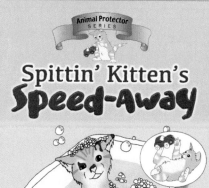

About Who Chains You Books

At Who Chains You, we publish books for those who believe people—and animals—deserve to be free

Who Chains You Publishing brings you books that educate, entertain, and share gripping plights of the animals we serve and those who rescue and stand in their stead.

We offer all kinds of stories about all kinds of animals: dogs, cats, rats, cows, pigeons, horses, pigs, snails, and so many more to come!

Visit our site and read more about us at whochainsyou.com.